River Has A Purpose

AND so... do... You!

Bethany Van Meter

illustrated by John Whitworth

The Library of Congress has cataloged the
paperback version as follows:

River has a Purpose and so do you!
Van Meter, Bethany.

Written by Bethany Van Meter
Illustrations by John Whitworth

Published in 2024 by Brandrock Studios

Dedicated to anyone who has supported or encouraged our journey as a family...to anyone who has taken the time to stop and help someone in need...to my husband, Josh, who has ALWAYS supported my dreams and has a heart for animals like I do...to my kids for inspiring me to write...to River...for bringing JOY to the masses...to God for His Provision...I am humbled beyond measure!

I see with my heart...
...because I have no eyes. They were removed, but it's alright.

I get funny looks.
Often people stare.

I know they're curious...
...sometimes they're scared!

Some are startled,
confused, and concerned.
Quickly they realize
there's something to learn!

SUBSTITUTE TEACHER:
River
TEACHER

That there's no need to worry...
and no need to fret.

My time on earth isn't finished just yet.

From homeless
to rooted,
and from sick
to healed

At this point you can tell
I haven't missed one meal!

I play soccer with my brothers.
My style is on trend.

The cat I got for Christmas?
Yeah, he's my best friend.

My family takes me to
Libraries, schools, and the like.

When I'm asked to come back to visit
We always say, " Alright!"

Kids are the BEST!
I LOVE to visit people.

I've even been to a place
that's topped with a steeple.

The connections I make
with people
Are my favorite,
I confess!

The lessons I teach
Are absolutely
Priceless!

I have so much

value,

even though

I'm **different,**

you see

People wag THEIR tails

When they see...

ME!

SAY CHEESE!
AWE! WHAT A CUTE PUPPY!
Good Boy!
COOL DOG!

So...
The next time you see someone,
(Two-legged or four)

Who may be different,
Try to learn more.

I WONDER HOW MUCH BUTTER I CAN EAT?
LIBRARY
Knowledge
Is
Power!

...and kindness
a fruit

You may even
make a
friend...

...whose LOVE is proof!

The End

Meet River!